Using
VALUES
to turn
VISION
into
REALITY

Bud Bilanich

FRONT ROW PRESS
Denver, Colorado

To Cathy

As Always

TABLE OF CONTENTS

PREFACE

The butterfly on this book's cover symbolizes transformation.

Just as caterpillars transform themselves into butterflies through metamorphosis, organizations can transform themselves through the use of Vision and Values.

This book is designed to assist people in leadership positions transform their organizations through the use of Vision and Values. Simply put, a "Vision" is a graphic description of a post transformation organization. "Values" are enduring principles which, when put into action, can drive an organizational metamorphosis.

I hope you'll find the ideas in this book to be exciting, helpful and easy to use. Good luck as you embark upon your journey of organizational transformation.

INTRODUCTION

INTRODUCTION

One can hardly pick up a management book these days that does not mention the term *Vision*. Most management writers encourage both individuals and organizations to develop a Vision in order to reach their full potential.

Many organizations have done this — only to find little or no change in how they operate or, more importantly, their bottom line. They can't get a handle on the "vision thing."

A simple baseball metaphor explains why.

Organizations who are dissatisfied with the results of their Vision efforts are leaving too many men on base.

INTRODUCTION

Most organizations leave men on base when it comes to Vision. Think of the situation in this way.

You get to first base when you develop a Vision. Many organizations stop here — leaving a man on first.

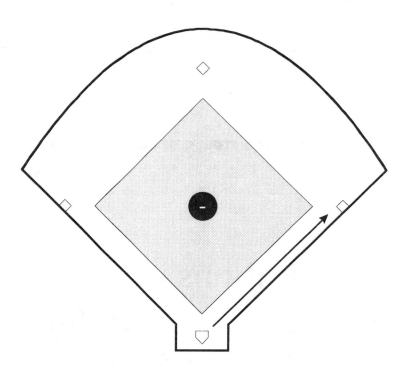

Organizations that do nothing more than develop a Vision statement have wasted their time and energy. Nothing will change if they do not address the next three steps.

INTRODUCTION

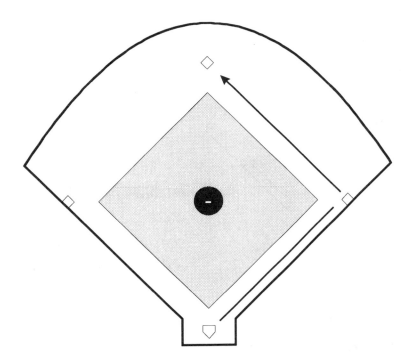

You move on to second base when you do an effective job of communicating your Vision to everyone in the organization.

Just as doubles are exciting in baseball; bright, glitzy communication events are nice to see, but don't result in any runs. If you stop here, you've left a man on second. The real work is merely started. In fact, you are only half way home.

INTRODUCTION

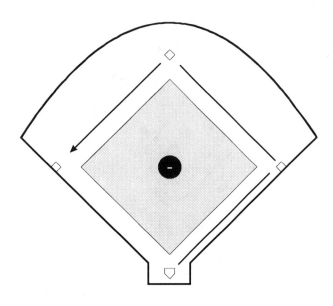

You get to third when you have aligned your organization's policies, procedures and systems with your Vision.

In baseball, you get to third base by hitting a triple — something unusual and calling for a lot of effort, or by being advanced by the hitters behind you — a difficult process requiring a lot of coordination between players.

However, a man on third has not scored a run. Expending the individual effort to hit a triple, or coordinating the process of moving a runner ahead is a frustrating experience if the runner is ultimately left on third base.

This is hard work, which requires a willingness to examine, and sometimes change practices that have served the organization well in the past. It takes courage to successfully complete step 3 of the Vision process.

However, organizations and the people who lead them, who are willing to face up to and change the inconsistencies in what they say and do, are the real winners in the long run.

INTRODUCTION

You score when you have developed a Vision, done an excellent job of communicating it, aligned your organizational policies procedures and systems with it, and have "actualized" it in your organization.

By actualizing your Vision, you will have left no men on base. You will have taken advantage of the power of Vision.

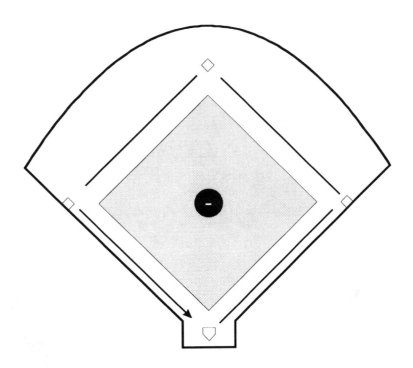

INTRODUCTION

Your vision is actualized when:

◆ People ACTUALLY speak about the Vision articulately,

◆ People ACTUALLY use the Vision to guide their day-to-day behavior,

◆ The Vision is ACTUALLY something about which people feel passionately,

◆ The Vision is ACTUALLY woven into the fabric of your organization.

INTRODUCTION

Many management books focus on getting you to first base — they tell you how to go about developing a Vision.

Some will help you get to second — they'll tell you how to communicate your Vision.

A few will guide you to third base — they'll provide you with advice on how to align your organization's policies, procedures and systems with your Vision.

Here, you'll learn how to score. You'll learn how to actualize your organization's vision. You'll learn a little about moving from first to second to third, but we'll concentrate on getting you home with that winning run.

INTRODUCTION
A Word About "Words"

In this book, the word "Vision" is used to describe a concept which has several parts. As it is used here, "Vision" has at least four distinct parts:

Purpose	The organization's fundamental reason for existing.
Mission	A statement of the organization's desired future.
Values	Core beliefs that guide decision making in the organization.
Vivid Description	A word picture that describes what the organization will be like when it fulfills its mission.

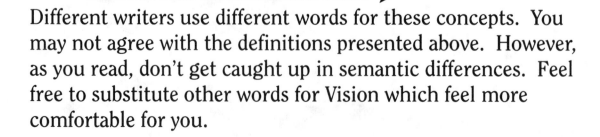

Different writers use different words for these concepts. You may not agree with the definitions presented above. However, as you read, don't get caught up in semantic differences. Feel free to substitute other words for Vision which feel more comfortable for you.

CHAPTER ONE

Developing a Vision

DEVELOPING A VISION
Part 1 — Drafting a Vision

Developing a Vision is simple in concept, but difficult in practice.

In general, developing a Vision has four steps:

1 -   Draft a Vision statement
2 -   Give it a reality check
3 -   Revise it
4 -   Get everyone to buy into it

Usually, a task team develops the Vision. This team should represent a cross section of the organization. It may include several organizational levels. However, visioning is a leadership function. So, in most cases, the task team is comprised of fairly senior members of the organization.

DEVELOPING A VISION

The team should begin by assessing the current situation — asking its members such questions as:

- How did we get to where we are today? What is our history? What did our founders stand for or believe in?

- What opportunities do we have currently? What threats are we facing?

- What are our current strengths and weaknesses?

- What are the critical issues we are facing regarding the future?

Once this assessment is complete, work can begin on writing the Purpose, Values, Mission and Vivid Description statements.

Developing a Vision

Purpose

To develop a Purpose statement ask: "Why does this organization exist?" If the best answer you can come up with is to "make money" or "maximize shareholder value," go back and try again.

In their best selling book *Built to Last*, Jim Collins and Jerry Porras say:

> *"An effective purpose captures the soul of an organization. Purpose gets at the deeper reasons for an organization's existence beyond just making money."*

Effective Purpose statements answer the questions "What do we do? and why do we do it?"

The role of a Purpose statement is to guide and inspire the organization for the long term.

DEVELOPING A VISION

MISSION

A Mission, on the other hand, is a statement of the organization's desired future.

> To develop a Mission statement ask:
>
> ◆ "Where are we going?"
>
> ◆ "What do we hope to accomplish over the next 10 years?"
>
> ◆ "What will we look like once we get there?"

A good Mission statement describes the future you plan on creating for the organization.

DEVELOPING A VISION

MISSION

To develop a Mission, you can focus both internally and externally. Internally focused Missions usually specify quantitative or qualitative targets like the GE Mission, *"Become number one of number two in every market we serve"* or Wal-Mart's Mission, written in 1990, *"Become a $125 billion company by the year 2000."*

Externally focused Missions usually emphasize on beating a specific competitor or emulating a role model. For example, in the 1960s, Nike developed a simple Mission, *"Crush Adidas."* In the 1940s, Stanford University developed the Mission, *"Become the Harvard of the West."*

DEVELOPING A VISION

VALUES

Values complement the Purpose and Mission by providing a set of principles which guide the behavior of everyone in the organization.

Organizational values are principles held in high esteem by all members of the organization. They provide meaning and identity for everyone's work life. They set parameters for decision making, and provide a rationale for individual and organizational actions and decisions.

It's best to discover rather than invent values. Look inside your organization. What are the enduring principles that are of vital importance to everyone in the organization? These are your core values.

Obviously, there is no right or wrong set of core values. Words like *"Integrity, Creativity, Teamwork, Communication, Customer Service, Quality, Personal and Professional Growth"* are often found in Values statements.

These may or may not be the values which guide your organization. The important thing is to identify the unique set of operating principles which guide behavior in your organization and allow you to achieve your Purpose.

DEVELOPING A VISION

VIVID DESCRIPTION

A Vivid Description complements the Mission by filling in the blanks. It is a word picture of what things will be like once the Mission is achieved. It should be engaging and compelling — something about which everyone in the organization can get excited. A good Vivid Description is a picture of the future which people can carry around in their heads.

To create a Vivid Description, begin by brainstorming a list of descriptive words which will be indicative of the way things will be. Refine the list, and then put it into a statement everyone will remember.

DEVELOPING A VISION

VIVID DESCRIPTION

In 1952 Archibald Carey, a civil rights activist and clergyman, said:

> *From every mountainside, let freedom ring.*
> *Not only from the Green Mountains of Vermont and New Hampshire; not only from the Catskills of New York; but from the Ozarks in Arkansas, or from the Stone Mountains in Georgia, from the Blue Ridge Mountains of Virginia.*
> *From every mountainside, let freedom ring.*

In his famous speech at the Lincoln Memorial, Dr. Martin Luther King, Jr. paraphrased these words:

> *Let freedom ring from Stone Mountain, Georgia.*
> *Let freedom ring from Lookout Mountain of Tennessee.*
> *Let freedom ring from every mountain and molehill in Mississippi.*
> *From every mountainside, let freedom ring.*

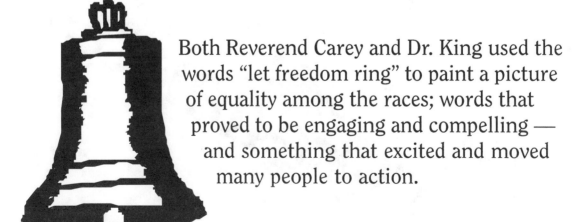

Both Reverend Carey and Dr. King used the words "let freedom ring" to paint a picture of equality among the races; words that proved to be engaging and compelling — and something that excited and moved many people to action.

DEVELOPING A VISION

VIVID DESCRIPTION

A Vivid Description, by its very nature, should appeal to the emotional side of organizational members. A pharmaceutical company plant manager used these words to launch a major safety initiative:

Everyone who works at this plant needs to be fanatical about safety. We need to care enough about each other to make sure that everybody works safely all the time.

Notice the use of the emotional words — *"fanatical"* and *"care enough about each other."* They paint a word picture of what the future has in store for those who work in that plant.

21

DEVELOPING A VISION
Part 2 — Reality Check

Once the Purpose, Mission, Values and Vivid Description have been developed by a group of senior managers, a reality check is necessary. Focus groups, comprised of a cross section of employees, are a good way to test the statements.

Be careful here, as this can get tricky. People in focus groups should be asked for broad conceptual input on the ideas expressed in the statements. However, these groups often want to provide specific feedback on the wording of the statements. This problem can be averted by skillful facilitation.

DEVELOPING A VISION
Part 3 — Revision

After receiving input from the organization via focus groups, the task team should revise the Purpose, Mission, Values and Vivid Description, incorporating any key thoughts which have been missed in the original draft. Task teams can — and do — suffer from groupthink. Most find input from focus groups to be very helpful.

The intent of all this work is not to write the *perfect* Purpose, Mission, Values and Vivid Description. Rather, the purpose is for senior leaders in the organization to think through the issues surrounding each of these statements to decide the direction to take the organization.

This work of specifying a direction for the organization is the essence of leadership. The people who make up an organization must know its purpose, fundamental values and future direction if they are to contribute effectively. Leaders have the responsibility for setting this direction.

DEVELOPING A VISION
Part 4 — Complete Buy In

The senior leader of the organization must completely and totally buy into the output of the task team. After all the drafts have been completed, he should carefully review the material to ensure complete comfort with it. If not, the leader should offer suggestions for changes.

In most cases, this buy-in step is a formality as most leaders prefer to either participate on the task team, or keep in touch via progress reports during the development process. Therefore, there is usually little to discuss or change. However, differences can arise at this late stage. In this case, the team should defer to the leader as he is the ultimate "owner" of the Purpose, Values, Mission and Vivid Description.

Once you've done these four tasks, you've successfully completed the first step in the vision process.

CHAPTER 2

Communicating the Vision

COMMUNICATING THE VISION

All of the work necessary to develop a Vision is only the beginning. An effective communication program is the next step. Organizational communication experts say there are two tools necessary for effective communication of a Vision:

- ♦ Multiple Channels of Communication

- ♦ Repetition

Channels are the vehicles by which information is communicated.

People receive and process information differently. Some people retain information best when they have an opportunity to read it. Others retain information better when they hear a presentation or watch a video. Still others retain information better if they have had a chance to discuss it with colleagues. That is why multiple channels of communication are so important.

COMMUNICATING THE VISION

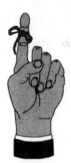  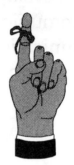  

Research has shown that people retain information they hear over and over. Late night television is a perfect example of this concept at work. Most commercials review the features and benefits of the product being sold, and then encourage you to purchase the product by calling a toll-free number. They will repeat this number several times. Also, the same commercial is likely to run two or three times an hour.

This is repetition at work. The viewer sees the same commercial several times in a concentrated time period, and hears the words "call now 800-222-2222" over and over. As annoying as these commercials are, they have been proven to be highly effective in selling products.

COMMUNICATING THE VISION

Multiple channels and repetition are the two keys to success in a Vision communication effort. These two concepts should be used in concert. They reinforce one another.

Below is a list of typical channels which can be used in a Vision communication effort.

- *Special Events* — Large meetings attended by the majority of organization members.

- *Newsletters* — Publications designed especially for the Vision communication, or articles in established publications within the organization.

- *Company Intranet* — Information about the Vision sent to every member of the organization electronically.

- *Letters Home* — Letters sent to the homes of all members of the organization containing information about the Vision.

COMMUNICATING THE VISION

♦ *Company Bulletins* — One-sheet publications distributed to all members of the organization at their workstations.

♦ *Videos* — Continuous loop videos detailing information about the Vision shown in public places (cafeteria, lobby etc.) in the organization.

♦ *Posters and Signs* — Information about the Vision prominently displayed throughout the organization.

♦ *Company Bulletin Boards* — One-sheet announcements placed on official organization bulletin boards.

♦ *Take Aways* — Small items used by members of the organization everyday, emblazoned with information regarding the Vision. For example:

- Pens and pencils
- Post-it notes
- Tablets and writing pads
- Mouse pads
- Screen savers
- Business card holders
- Desk stand cards
- Insulated lunch carry alls
- T-shirts, golf shirts, caps, other apparel
- Sporting goods (golf balls, tennis balls, Frisbees, etc.)
- Hot and cold drink cups
- Key chains
- Small flash lights

This list of channels and take aways is by no means exhaustive. Creative people in organizations often come up with many interesting and different ideas.

Communicating The Vision

All the channels mentioned (and others that you may develop) should be used to communicate the message of your Vision. Obviously some are very overt including special events, and letters home while some are more subliminal such as posters, signs and take aways.

The important point to remember here is that no one channel will suffice when you are communicating a Vision. Multiple channels are necessary if you are going to succeed.

Effective use of multiple communication channels results in use of the other tool - repetition. If you use multiple channels effectively, people will see the same message as often as 100 times per day. They will see posters and signs as they walk around their work area. Every time they use their computer mouse, they will think of the Vision. As they eat lunch, they might view the Vision video. Every time they pick up a pen or attach a Post-it note, they will be exposed to the message of the Vision.

Get the Vision's message to people in as many ways as possible, as often as possible.

CHAPTER 3

Aligning Organizational Practices

ALIGNING ORGANIZATIONAL PRACTICES

Developing and communicating a Vision is a lot of work. However, at this point, you're only half way into a successful Vision process. Your next job is to align organizational practices with the Vision. This requires conducting an exhaustive review of organizational policies, procedures and systems.

ALIGNING ORGANIZATIONAL PRACTICES

Often organizational policies, procedures and systems are out of alignment with the Vision. Let's look at some examples.

Many organizations say they value teamwork. However, their compensation system is set up to encourage individual accomplishment.

Trust and integrity are values that appear in many organizations' Visions. Yet these same organizations often require their employees to provide expense receipts for amounts as small as a dollar.

Still other organizations proclaim to want leaders who will manage for the long term and build the culture of the organization. However, they promote solely on the basis of financial performance or technical competence.

Finally, many organizations claim to value a diverse workforce, yet they continue to recruit from the sources they have always used.

ALIGNING ORGANIZATIONAL PRACTICES

Organizations are not consciously attempting to sabotage their Vision. In most cases they probably have not even realized that their policies, procedures and systems are not in alignment with it.

Organizations that are serious about their Vision must be willing to review and, if necessary, change the policies, procedures and systems under which they have operated for years. This is not an easy task. It begins with a willingness to review and challenge paradigms that have served the organization well in the past.

Once misaligned policies, procedures and systems are identified, they must be changed. In their book *Built to Last*, Jim Collins and Jerry Porras offer a succinct, but powerful suggestion:

Obliterate
Misalignments

ALIGNING ORGANIZATIONAL PRACTICES

Where do you look for misalignments? Some of the best places are:

- ◆ Compensation Policies
- ◆ Selection and Promotion Practices
- ◆ Required Reports
- ◆ Training Programs — Management, Leadership and Technical
- ◆ Orientation Programs
- ◆ Employee Relations Policies and Procedures
- ◆ Performance Management Programs
- ◆ Perks Program

The list is almost without limits.

Identifying and "obliterating" misalignments is an ongoing process. True Visionary organizations are constantly on the lookout for policies, procedures, systems and practices that are not aligned with their espoused Vision.

Identifying and changing misaligned practices is not something done once and forgotten. Rather, organizations that are willing to hold themselves and their practices up to close scrutiny will constantly find new opportunities for creating better alignment.

Aligning Organizational Practices

Often, misalignments are in an isolated part of the organization.

Sometimes, they are company wide.

Regardless of where they are found, organizational practices that do not support or, worse yet, conflict with the Vision must be changed.

Misalignments result in cynicism and skepticism among organizational members. They undermine leaders' credibility.

Organizations, and those who lead them, must be congruent in what they say and do. Saying one thing and doing another, results in a situation where the people who make up an organization doubt the sincerity of any organizational initiative.

In the best case, they adopt a wait-and-see attitude. In the worst case, they refuse to support organizational initiatives until they are coerced into doing so. Commitment given grudgingly is half-hearted at best.

CHAPTER 4

Using Values to Actualize the Vision

ACTUALIZING THE VISION

Organizations that successfully implement the concepts described in the previous section have taken a major step in becoming driven by their Vision.

However, there is still a lot of work to be done. To return to our baseball metaphor, organizations that develop and communicate a Vision, and then align their policies and practices with it, have merely gotten to third base. To score, they need to "Actualize" their vision. Organizational values are the key.

ACTUALIZING THE VISION

Senior leaders play the most important role in *developing* and *communicating* their organization's Vision, and *aligning* its practices with it.

Mid, lower level and informal leaders play the most significant role in *actualizing* it.

> # Values are their primary tool.

Organizational values provide the direction organizations need to make their Vision a reality. Values are enduring concepts held in high esteem by everyone in an organization. They are guiding principles for day-to-day decision making, providing direction for organizational members in ambiguous situations. Besides guiding decision making, values provide a rationale for actions taken by an organization and its members.

Just as most people have a set of personal values that guide decision making in their personal lives, organizational values should be used to guide their decision making at work.

ACTUALIZING THE VISION

There are five conditions that must exist for an organization to be values driven and achieve its Vision:

1 Everyone in the organization must *understand and accept* the values.

2 Everyone in the organization must *know what they should do* to act in a manner consistent with the values.

3 Everyone in the organization should be *recognized and rewarded* for operating in a manner consistent with the values.

4 Everyone in the organization must *experience negative consequences* for acting in a manner inconsistent with the values.

5 There must be *no obstacles* to acting in a manner consistent with the values.

ACTUALIZING THE VISION

Leaders have a direct impact on each of these conditions. To impact these conditions in a positive way, leaders must possess and use three skills:

1. Modeling Appropriate Behavior
2. Conducting of Work Group Meetings
3. Interacting One to One

Prior to discussing how the skills and conditions are related, let's look at each condition and skill in more detail.

CHAPTER 5

*Identifying Conditions to Achieve
Your Vision*

CONDITION 1:
Understanding and Acceptance

Before most people are willing to support organizational values, they want to have a complete understanding of them. In most cases, they want to know the answers to the following types of questions:

- Why is there such a big focus on vision and values now?

- Where did this vision and these values come from?

- Who decided to go in this direction?

- Why?

- How is this different from what we've been doing?

- What's expected of me?

- Is this something on which I should spend my valuable time and energy?

CONDITION 1:
Understanding and Acceptance

Understanding is a cognitive process. Its focus is information. Creating understanding is easier than creating acceptance — an emotional process.

Understanding is focused on the rational; acceptance depends on the non-rational. To put it another way, one promotes understanding by appealing to the head, and acceptance by appealing to the heart.

A comprehensive, multi-channel communication program is likely to result in understanding.

Acceptance takes much more. It begins with understanding, as it is difficult for anyone to accept something that he or she does not completely understand.

Acceptance, however, goes further. For someone to truly accept organizational vision and values, he or she must feel comfortable with them. One can understand a concept completely, but not accept it.

CONDITION 1:
Understanding and Acceptance

Acceptance deals with the following types of questions:

- Do I agree with the vision and values?
- Are they in line with my values and beliefs?
- Are they good for me personally?
- Are they good for the company?
- Do I trust the company to do what they're asking me to do?

The best way to address acceptance issues is to confront them head on. When people are feeling somewhat uncomfortable with an idea, they have lots of questions.

Often, these questions are interpreted as resistance. Resistance is often met with frustration or contempt — which leads to more questions. Leaders must accept questions with an open mind, not label those who ask them as being resistant.

Often, people who ask questions for clarification are treated by their leaders as if they are being resistant. This, in turn, leads them to become suspicious — and more resistant.

CONDITION 1:
Understanding and Acceptance

Therefore, to help people accept organizational values, leaders should:

◆ Answer all questions about the values.

◆ Let people vent.

◆ Then gently nudge them towards developing positive suggestions for using the values as a guide to their decision making.

CONDITION 2:
Knowing What To Do

One of the biggest mistakes leaders make is assuming that people know: a) what is expected of them, and b) how to do the things which are expected.

Leaders often take the approach "I don't have to tell them what to do; they should know what to do." This is a mistake. In most cases, assumptions lead to trouble. When it comes to performance expectations, assumptions can be very costly.

The same holds true for values. Often, leaders assume that because values have been published and people have attended a communication meeting, they know what to do to conduct themselves in a manner consistent with the values. Wrong. Values like Innovation, Customer Focus, Respect for the Individual, Community and Integrity are merely abstract concepts to most people. For them to become part of the fabric of an organization, leaders must take the time to ensure that people not only know what the values are, but understand the specific, concrete behaviors which are expected of them if they are to live up to the values.

53

CONDITION 2:
Knowing What To Do

This translation process — from abstract concept to concrete behavior — must be directed by leaders. Leaders have three tools at their disposal: their own behavior, work group meetings, and one to one discussions. Through the skillful application of these tools, leaders can ensure that people not only know *what* to do to act in accordance with the values, but *how* to do it.

A strong, positive example is the most powerful tool for influencing the behavior of others. In their book *Walk the Talk,* Eric Harvey and Al Lucia make the following point:

You earn the right to expect others to do things by doing those things yourself.

CONDITION 2:
Knowing What To Do

However, a strong example is not always enough. Leaders should not assume that because they act in accordance with their organization's values that others will automatically follow their lead. Successful leaders not only model appropriate behavior, they explain their actions.

For example, a leader in an organization that held communication as a value often made the following statement in response to a question regarding whether certain information should be made public:

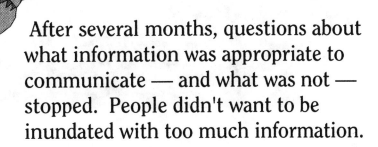

"We say we value communication, so we're going to communicate this information to everybody. If we are going to err, I want to err on the side of providing too much information, not too little."

After several months, questions about what information was appropriate to communicate — and what was not — stopped. People didn't want to be inundated with too much information.

CONDITION 2:
Knowing What To Do

Successful leaders also use meetings and one to one
discussions to ensure that people understand the specific
things they can do to make their organization's vision and
values a reality. Open, frank discussions about the values and
behaviors associated with them are keys to success.

CONDITION 3:
Rewards and Recognition

Jerry McGuire was a hit movie in 1996. Long after it is forgotten, people will still remember its most famous line: "SHOW ME THE MONEY."

Many leaders mistakenly believe that the only way to reward people is by showing them the money. Often, they feel frustrated because their organizations' compensation policies severely limit their ability to use money as a reward. However, money is but one form of recognition. Leaders who cannot control financial rewards to the extent they might like need to focus on what they *can* control.

CONDITION 3:
Rewards and Recognition

Most people tune into radio station WII FM, or "What's In It For Me?"

We all like a pat on the back or a kind word now and then. Leaders can use this to their advantage by recognizing and rewarding people who act in a manner consistent with the values. Leaders have two opportunities for rewarding and recognizing people who live up to organizational values.

Most people are consistently good performers and will do what is expected of them. These individuals should be recognized for their efforts.

Second, occasionally a leader will encounter an individual who has gone to extraordinary lengths to live a particular value. This type of effort calls for recognition also.

CONDITION 3:
Rewards and Recognition

Outstanding individual efforts and/or consistently good performance must be reinforced if they are to continue.

Most people do not need constant reinforcement, but almost everyone needs and appreciates a sincere thank you for their efforts on occasion.

CONDITION 3:
Rewards and Recognition

Leaders can reinforce organizational values by providing the people who have demonstrated a commitment to acting in accordance with them with specific, sincere feedback. Merely telling an individual that he or she has "done a good job on the values" is not enough. Leaders must pinpoint what the person did, how it relates to and reinforces the values, and why it is important to both the work group and company.

This feedback should also be timely. Positive reinforcement that follows on the heels of a particular action is much more effective than feedback given later in a performance review.

CONDITION 3:
Rewards and Recognition

*People do
things
that get them
rewarded.*

CONDITION 4:
Negative Consequences

The reverse is also true. Even in the best companies, a small number of people will act in ways that are inconsistent with organizational values. The reasons for this behavior are varied. However, these two stand out:

1)   People don't know they are acting in a manner inconsistent with the values.

2)   They know they are not acting in accordance with the values, but see no reason to change their behavior.

Just as people should experience positive consequences for doing the right thing, they should experience negative consequences for refusing to do so.

CONDITION 4:
Negative Consequences

If people truly do not realize that their behavior is inconsistent with organizational values, leaders need to tell them. This is a rather easy and straightforward process. Most people want to do the right thing, and will accept and use feedback that heightens their awareness of the impact of their behavior.

CONDITION 4:
Negative Consequences

However, occasionally leaders will encounter people who know their behavior is inconsistent with organizational values but choose not to change it. In these cases, leaders must take on the unpleasant task of attempting to change behavior through the use of negative consequences.

Negative consequences range from things like discipline (up to and including termination) to the absence or withholding of positive consequences like raises and promotions.

For example, "empowerment" is a value in many organizations. On occasion, an organization which holds empowerment as a value may find that a manager with an excellent track record of delivering bottom-line results achieves them by micro managing people and driving them to the point of exhaustion. If this manager receives the feedback that his or her actions are not in line with company values and still refuses to change, negative consequences follow. These negative consequences could take the form of a lower-than-expected raise or not receiving an expected promotion.

CONDITION 4:
Negative Consequences

This discussion of negative consequences is not meant to imply that organizations should develop a punitive attitude regarding their values.

However, people who simply don't care if they conduct themselves in a manner consistent with organizational values benefit from feeling some pressure to do so.

Negative consequences need not be heavy handed. Most people usually need only a gentle reminder — a tap on the shoulder and a brief discussion — to get them back on track.

CONDITION 4:
Negative Consequences

Negative consequences play another role. They send a signal to the entire organization that the values are important, and that everyone is expected to conduct themselves in a manner consistent with them. Judicious use of negative consequences makes it clear to all members of an organization that how you do your work — living by values — is just as important as what you accomplish.

CONDITION 5:
No Obstacles

Obstacles most often arise because of alignment problems. When organizational practices are not aligned with organizational values, people have a difficult time conducting themselves in a manner consistent with the values. Some examples follow.

CONDITION 5
No Obstacles

AN EXAMPLE

A credit card issuing bank holds customer service as a value. It has gone to great lengths in its marketing materials to proclaim that "Customer Service is Our Number 1 Priority." Employees are urged to "focus on the customer" and "do whatever it takes to create satisfied, loyal customers." However, many employees complain that the bank's policies and procedures make it impossible for them to provide good customer service.

They cite the following example. Occasionally a customer's payment will not be credited to his account. In this case, the customer is asked to provide a copy of the canceled check as proof of payment. Most customers are willing to provide the necessary documentation. However, once they have done so they expect the bank to credit their account.

The bank, however, has a policy stating that no credit can be made to a customer's account until a corresponding debit has been posted to the account to which funds were erroneously applied. Therefore, customers are told that their account will not be credited until the bank determines the location of the misapplied funds. The bank is applying the age-old accounting maxim: "for every credit, there must be a corresponding debit."

Customers are not willing to accept this. In essence, the bank is saying, "We acknowledge the fact that we made an error. However, we will not fix your problem until we get our act together internally."

Customer Service Representatives are caught in the middle. They are attempting to provide excellent customer service, but find themselves hamstrung by a bank policy. The policy in question makes perfect sense from a financial control perspective. However, it undermines effective customer service.

In this case, bank leaders can identify a practice that will allow the bank to maintain effective financial controls, while providing Customer Service Representatives the ability to provide the level of service desired by its customers.

CONDITION 5:
No Obstacles

Organizations that are serious about their values make it easy for everyone to conduct themselves in a manner consistent with them by identifying and removing obstacles.

Typically, three types of situations create obstacles to successful application of organizational values. Each has a relatively simple solution.

SITUATION 1

♦ Policies, procedures and practices exist that prevent people from living in accordance with organizational values.

Address this situation by reviewing organizational practices and changing those that make it difficult for people to conduct themselves in a manner consistent with organizational values.

One company handled this situation by creating a "Stupid Policy Alert Form." Everyone in the organization was invited to identify policies that got in the way of doing the job effectively.

CONDITION 5:
No Obstacles

SITUATION 2

♦ People do not realize they have the wherewithal to remove or overcome an obstacle.

Address this situation by reinforcing and publicly recognizing people who take risks or go out of their way to conduct themselves in a manner consistent with organizational values.

SITUATION 3

♦ People do not have the skills necessary to conduct themselves in a manner consistent with organizational values.

Address this final situation by clarifying expectations and then providing people with the skills necessary for conducting themselves in a manner consistent with organizational values.

CHAPTER 6

Modeling Appropriate Behavior

LEADERSHIP SKILLS

Now that we've looked at the five conditions necessary for an organization to be values driven, let's turn our attention to leadership skills. There are three leadership skills necessary for success in creating a values driven organization:

◆ **Modeling Appropriate Behavior**

◆ **Conducting Work Group Meetings**

◆ **Interacting One to One**

MODELING APPROPRIATE BEHAVIOR

If people are to conduct themselves in a manner consistent with organizational values, they must observe their leaders doing the same. In *Walk the Talk*, Eric Harvey and Al Lucia point out:

People Hear What We Say And See What We Do, And Seeing Is Believing

MODELING APPROPRIATE BEHAVIOR

In other words, leaders must not only support organizational values verbally, they must conduct themselves in a manner consistent with those values at all times.

Leaders are under a microscope. People around leaders are always alert to what they are doing. They watch what leaders do, and often model their own behavior on what they have observed. They watch to see if and how stated organizational values influence the actions of leaders.

The message is clear. If leaders expect people to conduct themselves in a manner consistent with organizational values, they need to do so themselves.

MODELING APPROPRIATE BEHAVIOR

Leaders who do what they say are perceived as credible. Leadership credibility is a key factor in creating a values-driven organization. Leaders can enhance their credibility by responding appropriately at what Jan Carlzon, President of Scandinavian Airlines, describes as "moments of truth."

For leaders, every interaction — with a colleague, employee, vendor, customer, or other constituent — is a moment of truth. Leader actions at these moments of truth either make or break their credibility with the people around them.

The Challenge Is Not To Find Better Values, But To Be Faithful To Those We Profess.

John Gardner,
Founder, Common Cause

MODELING APPROPRIATE BEHAVIOR

It's important to understand that values are intangibles — one cannot see a value. However, people can and do observe leadership behavior. Leadership behavior is how values manifest themselves.

As children, most of us were exposed to the science experiment in which a magnet was placed into some iron filings. The filings immediately arranged themselves in a pattern around the magnet. What we saw was the manifestation of the 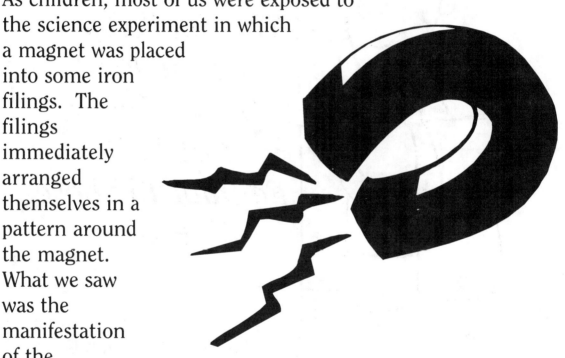 magnetic field — not the actual field, which is something that is not observable.

The same is true of values. Values cannot be observed. However, their results can be — and are — everyday. People watch what their leaders do, and compare this behavior to their organization's values.

MODELING APPROPRIATE BEHAVIOR

In *The Leadership Challenge,* Jim Kouzes and Barry Posner focus on the concept of values as intangibles:

> *Values are intangibles. In marketing intangibles, organizations know they must make them tangible to the customer. The only way leaders can make organizational values tangible and real to followers is through their behavior and actions.*

MODELING APPROPRIATE BEHAVIOR

One of the most well known examples of organizational leaders walking their talk and making organizational values tangible occurred in 1982.

Seven people died after ingesting Extra Strength Tylenol capsules. The product had been tampered with on store shelves. Cyanide had been added to some capsules. The senior management of Johnson and Johnson, the company who makes and sells Tylenol, acted quickly and decisively. They recalled and destroyed all the Tylenol on the shelves in stores all over the United States — more than $100 million of product. When asked if this was a difficult decision, CEO James Burke replied:

> *"No. Our Credo (Johnson and Johnson's organizational values) says 'our first responsibility is to the doctors, nurses, and patients, to mothers and all others who use our products'. The decision was easy. If there was the slightest possibility that even one other person would suffer adverse consequences as a result of using our product, we would not be living up to our Credo. So we pulled the product. We'd do it again in a similar situation."*

MODELING APPROPRIATE BEHAVIOR

To create a values-driven organization, leaders must consciously focus people's attention and behaviors. They can do this by intentionally modeling organizational values until they become standard operating procedure, or "the way we do things around here."

Modeling is especially important at "moments of truth." The message about what really counts must be delivered, demonstrated, pointed out and emphasized by each leader's actions. Leaders must consciously structure moments of truth to communicate and reinforce organizational values.

MODELING APPROPRIATE BEHAVIOR

Leaders can model behavior consistent with organizational values by focusing on the following five tools:

♦ How They Spend Their Time

♦ The Questions They Ask

♦ Their Reactions to Problems and Crises

♦ What They Reward

♦ What They Sanction or Punish

MODELING APPROPRIATE BEHAVIOR
Time

Time is the truest test of what leaders think is important. Once organizational values have been communicated, leaders can set a positive example merely by focusing their time and attention on them. If an organization says it values customers, leaders must focus some of their daily attention on meeting customer needs — whether internal or external.

By the same token, in organizations that say they value innovation, leaders must ask people to focus on better ways of doing things, and reward them for taking appropriate risks —

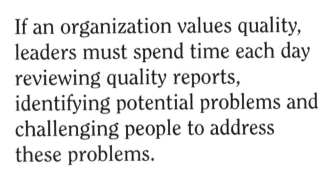

even if the results were less than what was hoped for.

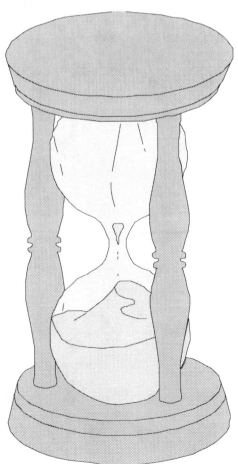

If an organization values quality, leaders must spend time each day reviewing quality reports, identifying potential problems and challenging people to address these problems.

The concept is simple. However, like many good ideas, the genius is in the doing, not the thinking.

MODELING APPROPRIATE BEHAVIOR

Spend Your Time On What You Say Is Important

MODELING APPROPRIATE BEHAVIOR
Questions

Questions point people in the right direction. They send messages about the leader's focus. To create a values-driven organization, leaders must ask questions that pertain to organizational values. For example:

In an organization that values Teamwork, leaders should ask questions like:

"Have you checked with the Sales Department on this?" or "That's a great idea. Who might be negatively affected by it?"

In an organization that values Community, leaders might ask questions like:

"How will this affect the people who live near our facility?" or "Which community groups are most deserving of our support and limited resources?"

Or, in an organization that values Performance, leaders might ask questions like:

"What effect will this idea have on our bottom line?" or "Will this idea help us meet our budgeted targets?"

By asking the correct questions, leaders show those around them what is important. Leaders who use organizational values to formulate the questions they ask set a positive model which goes a long way in creating a truly values-driven organization.

MODELING APPROPRIATE BEHAVIOR
Reactions to Problems and Crises

Problems and crises present another opportunity for leaders to model behavior consistent with organizational values. In fact, they point out the truth or fiction of the importance of organizational values. In times of stress, people often show their true colors. If leaders react to problems and crises in a manner that reinforces organizational values, those values are likely to become part of the fabric of the organization.

If they react in a manner that conflicts with organizational values, people will come to regard the values as unimportant. The Johnson and Johnson Tylenol tampering case is a very good example of leaders acting in a manner consistent with organizational values in a crisis. By their actions, leaders at Johnson and Johnson sent an unmistakably clear, loud message to people inside and outside of the company of the importance of the Johnson & Johnson Credo in conducting day-to-day business.

MODELING APPROPRIATE BEHAVIOR
Reactions to Problems and Crises

Let's look at other examples. If a company holds "respect for people" as one of its values, leaders must not engage in witch hunts every time a problem surfaces. They should focus on solving the problem, and not on punishing the person or persons responsible for it. This is not to say that poor performance should be overlooked or not addressed. Rather, leaders in an organization that values "respect for people" should use problems as an opportunity for learning — to prevent similar problems from arising in the future.

If a company holds "innovation" or "research and development" as a key value, leaders must continue to fund R&D efforts at a consistent level — in good times and bad. This is especially true in these days when company stock price is dramatically affected by quarterly results.

Resolve Problems And Crises By Focusing On Core Values.

MODELING APPROPRIATE BEHAVIOR
Rewards

Rewarding people who act in a manner consistent with values is one of the conditions necessary for being a values-driven organization. Rewards are also tools for leaders to send a message about the importance of organizational values.

For example, if an organization says it places a premium on innovation, its leaders should promote risk taking and innovative behavior by rewarding — with promotions, public recognition, increased responsibility — people, who take responsible risks and develop innovative solutions to problems.

MODELING APPROPRIATE BEHAVIOR
Sanctions and Punishment

While the appropriate use of rewards is an important condition for being a values-driven organization, the reverse is also true. The judicious application of negative consequences — sanctions and punishment — is equally important.

Organizations that value "empowerment and accountability," for example, should not reward technically competent and qualified people who have not demonstrated a willingness to delegate important tasks and responsibilities. If they do, they send the message that living in accordance with organizational values is not important.

It's sad but true. Some people will respond only to negative, not positive, consequences. These people need to feel the sting of disappointment associated with a lost opportunity or smaller pay increase before they are willing to get on board with organizational values.

MODELING APPROPRIATE BEHAVIOR

Sanctions and Punishment

Sanctions and punishments should be a last resort. Leaders who use these four tools . . .

- ◆ Attention to how they spend their time

- ◆ Questions which reinforce organizational values

- ◆ Appropriate reactions to problems and crises

- ◆ Rewarding behavior consistent with organizational values

. . . will not have to resort to sanctions and punishment often.

CHAPTER 7

Conducting Work Group Meetings

CONDUCTING WORK GROUP MEETINGS

Well-run meetings are one of the most effective tools a leader has in creating a values-driven organization. Effective leaders use two types of meetings to ensure that organizational values become a part of the fabric of their organization:

Communicating Values As Expectations

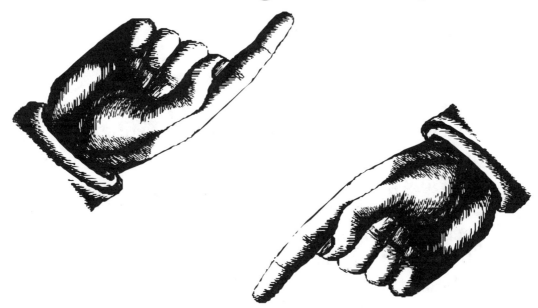

Values Action Planning

We will discuss each of these in detail. First, however, let's focus on the basic principles involved in conducting effective meetings. The outline on the next page illustrates the four elements and 13 steps of effective meetings.

13 STEPS TO BETTER MEETINGS

PREPARE

1   Plan the meeting — who, what, when, where and WHY.
2   Prepare an agenda — put items into a logical sequence.

INFORM

3   Check availability of key attendees.
4   Distribute the agenda in advance.

STRUCTURE AND CONTROL

5   Start on time.
6   Review and, if necessary, revise the agenda.
7   Review action items from previous meeting
    (if appropriate).
8   Unite the group:
    Encourage people to share their issues and concerns
9   Focus the group:
    Stick to the agenda.
10 Mobilize the group:
    Establish action items — who, what, when.
11 Set time, date and place of next meeting.

SUMMARIZE AND FOLLOW UP

12 Review, summarize and distribute action items.
13 Monitor progress on action items.

PREPARATION

All effective meetings begin with solid preparation. There are two steps in the preparation phase.

Planning

> Ask yourself:
>
> - ♦   **WHAT** needs to be accomplished in this meeting?
>
> - ♦   **WHO** needs to be here?
>
> - ♦   **WHEN** is the best time for the meeting?
>
> - ♦   **WHERE** is the best place for the meeting?

Agenda Setting

> Put the items you expect to cover in the meeting into a logical sequence. Assign time limits for each agenda item.

INFORMATION

Effective meetings have the right participants. There is nothing more frustrating for a group than to belatedly realize that a key person — someone with necessary information or decision-making authority — is not in attendance.

The people in attendance wisely arrive prepared to carry on a meaningful discussion. To do this, they should have received the agenda in advance of the meeting. In this way, they'll know how to prepare for the meeting and which information to bring with them.

Today's Meeting Agenda

People present:

Items for discussion:

 12:00 - 12:30:   Topic 1

  12:30 - 1:30:   Topic 2

   1:30 - 2:00:   Topic 3

STRUCTURE AND CONTROL

The preparation and information phases set the stage for the meeting. Once the meeting begins, it is important that it is structured and controlled properly. The best way to get any meeting started off properly is to begin on time. Then, people who are late get the message and will arrive on time for subsequent meetings.

The first item of business should be a review of the agenda. This is the time to make revisions if any are necessary. Then, if appropriate, action items from any previous meetings should be reviewed.

STRUCTURE AND CONTROL

In successful meetings, there is a feeling of cohesion and unity. The chief threats to cohesion and unity are aggression and infighting. Successful meeting leaders promote cohesion and unity by:

> ♦ Encouraging people to openly share their issues and concerns
> ♦ Not taking sides
> ♦ Involving everybody
> ♦ Focusing on facts — not opinions or generalizations

Second, successful meetings are focused. The chief threat to focus is a discussion that wanders and gets off the point. This is the downfall of most meetings. Successful meeting leaders maintain focus by:

> ♦ Bringing the discussion back to the point quickly
> ♦ Ensuring everyone understands comments and suggestions
> ♦ Periodically paraphrasing decisions and action items

Third, successful meetings result in action. The chief threat to action is the squashing of good ideas before they have been explored fully. Successful meeting leaders move to action by:

> ♦ Making sure everyone has an opportunity to present ideas
> ♦ Recording all suggestions
> ♦ Ensuring ideas do not get dismissed prematurely
> ♦ Using ideas as building blocks to establish action items

Finally, prior to adjourning, the time, date and place of the next meeting should be determined.

Summary And Follow Up

After a meeting, successful meeting leaders review, summarize and distribute action items from the meeting. They also follow up with meeting participants to monitor progress on action items. In this way, the next meeting will be off to a successful start.

This model is summarized on the next page.

13 STEPS TO BETTER MEETINGS

PREPARE	INFORM	STRUCTURE AND CONTROL	SUMMARIZE AND FOLLOW UP
Plan the meeting — who, what, when, where and WHY. Prepare an agenda — put items into a logical sequence.	Check availability of key attendees. Distribute the agenda in advance.	Start on time. Review and, if necessary, revise the agenda. Review action items from previous meeting (if appropriate). Unite the group: Encourage people to share their issues and concerns. Focus the group: Stick to the agenda. Mobilize the group: Establish action items — who, what, when. Set time, date and place of next meeting.	Review, summarize and distribute action items. Monitor progress on action items.

VALUES AND MEETINGS

As mentioned above, leaders in values-driven organizations regularly conduct two types of meetings:

Communicating Values as Expectations

Values Action Planning

The four step model . . .

- ♦ Prepare
- ♦ Inform
- ♦ Structure and Control
- ♦ Summarize and Follow up

. . . works for both of these types of meetings.

Meeting Guides for Communicating Values as Expectations, and Values Action Planning Meetings follow.

MEETING GUIDE
Communicating Values as Expectations

PREPARE

♦ Determine the time and location for the Departmental Values Communication Meeting.

♦ Review the values. Determine what each means to you personally. Outline a few comments which describe your view of each value.

♦ Write opening and closing statements for the meeting.

INFORM

♦ Check to ensure that everyone in the department will be available for the meeting.

♦ Using your typical means of communication, inform your people of where and when the meeting will take place.

STRUCTURE AND CONTROL

♦ Start on time.

♦ Open the meeting using the statement you prepared prior to the meeting.

♦ Describe the role values play in an effective organization.

♦ Review each value individually, focusing on what it means to you personally. Use the notes you prepared prior to the meeting.

♦ Ask the group if they understand the values. Answer any questions which arise.

♦ Tell the group that you will expect them to act in a manner consistent with the values.

♦ Tell the group that you are committed to the values. Invite them to give you feedback on your behavior regarding the values.

♦ Tell the group you are available to individually discuss any questions or concerns they may have regarding the values.

♦ Close the meeting using the statement you prepared prior to the meeting.

SUMMARIZE AND FOLLOW UP

♦ Distribute a written summary of the values and your personal commitments regarding them.

MEETING GUIDE

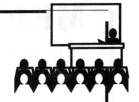

Values Action Planning

PREPARE

- ◆ Determine the time and location of the Action Planning Meeting.

- ◆ Review the value to be discussed at the meeting. Determine what it means to you personally. Evaluate your department's strengths and weaknesses in relation to this value. Outline a few comments on these topics.

- ◆ Write opening and closing statements for the meeting.

INFORM

- ◆ Check to ensure that everyone in the department will be available for the meeting.

- ◆ Using your typical means of communication, inform your people of where and when the meeting will take place.

STRUCTURE AND CONTROL

- ◆ Start on time.

- ◆ Open the meeting using the statement you prepared prior to the meeting. Tell the group:

  - • You are here to discuss the value.

  - • Your objective is to arrive at a consensus on a list of specific actions, to which you all commit. These action will result in your department acting in a manner consistent with this value.

  - • This is important. Specific commitments are more likely to result in the values becoming a part of everyday life of the department than vague, general statements of support.

- ◆ Review the value under discussion. Using the notes you prepared prior to the meeting, tell the group:

  - • Your personal beliefs and feelings regarding this value.

  - • Your assessment of your department's strengths and weaknesses regarding this value.

Meeting Guide continued on next page

MEETING GUIDE
Values Action Planning

- ♦ Ask the group:

    - • What are we currently doing which enhances this value? Record these answers on a flip chart titled "CONTINUE".

    - • What are we currently doing which detracts from or diminishes this value? Record these answers on a flip chart titled "STOP".

    - • What are we not doing currently but should do to enhance this value? Record these answers on a flip chart titled "START".

- ♦ Review the charts with group. Get clarification on any points of confusion.

- ♦ If appropriate, develop action plans for the "STOP" and "START" items.

- ♦ Record comments and issues regarding another department or management on a flip chart titled "ISSUES".

- ♦ Close the meeting with the statement you prepared prior to the meeting:

    - • Stress the importance of open, frank discussions regarding values.

    - • Indicate your commitment to the "CONTINUE", "STOP" and "START" actions.

    - • Indicate that you will discuss the items on the issues chart with the appropriate people.

    - • Thank the group for its participation.

SUMMARIZE AND FOLLOW UP

- ♦ Distribute a written summary of the "CONTINUE", "STOP" and "START" commitments to the group.

- ♦ Discuss and resolve the items on the "ISSUES" chart with the appropriate people.

- ♦ Inform your group in writing (or at the beginning of the next values action planning meeting) of the results of these conversations.

SUCCESSFUL MEETINGS

The Leader's Job is to Orchestrate the Meeting . . .

SUCCESSFUL MEETINGS

. . . NOT to Beat People
into Submission

CHAPTER 8

*Conducting Effective
One to One Interactions*

ONE TO ONE INTERACTION

Perhaps the greatest tool leaders have in making their organizations values driven is one to one discussions with people they work with every day. Simple conversations help them understand if they are conducting themselves in a manner consistent with organizational values.

Leaders should employ these two types of discussions with some frequency:

Reinforcing Behavior Consistent With Values

Redirecting Behavior Inconsistent With Values

Just as there is a generic model for conducting work group meetings, there is a simple four-step model for conducting successful one to one discussions.

12 STEPS TO SUCCESSFUL INTERACTIONS

OPENING

1   Explain reasons for discussion.
2   Explain importance of discussion.

INFORMATION SHARING

3   Seek information.
4   Give information.
5   Review and summarize information.

DECISION

6   Ask for suggestions.
7   Listen.
8   Build on suggestions.
9   Decide on plan of action.
10 Determine and assign responsibilities.

CLOSING

11 Summarize plan of action.
12 Set follow-up date.

OPENING

There are two objectives in this opening step. Make sure the individual with whom you are having the discussion understands the reasons for the discussion and its importance. Often, leaders skip or gloss over this step. This is a mistake.

Don't assume people realize why you are speaking with them, or why the topic of the discussion is important to you or your work group.

Stating the reason for a discussion and its importance gets things off to a good start by putting both people on an equal footing.

INFORMATION SHARING

The main objective of this Information Sharing step is to get all of the information regarding the situation being discussed out into the open. Effective leaders ask for the other person's perspective on the situation before giving their own. In this way, they avoid biasing the other's comments. Most people will say what they think their leaders want to hear. Therefore, by asking for information before giving their thoughts on the situation, leaders avoid receiving distorted or incomplete information.

After the information has been presented and discussed, successful leaders take the time to summarize before moving on to the next step. This summary provides an opportunity to identify any missing information and clarify any misperceptions.

DECISION

Just as in meetings, most one to one discussions result in some action. This action is determined in the Decision step. As in the previous step, successful leaders avoid biasing the other person's ideas by asking for his or her ideas first, and then building on those suggestions.

This step should result in a plan of action which clarifies the responsibilities of both people for carrying out the plan.

CLOSING

Successful leaders know that good discussions do not end abruptly. They close one to one discussions by summarizing the plan of action and setting a time to check progress on the plan. It's important to conclude discussions in a manner which results in both parties having a sense of closure and a clear idea of what happens next.

This model is summarized on the next page.

12 Steps to Successful Interactions

OPENING	INFORMATION SHARING	DECISION	CLOSING
Explain reasons for discussion. Explain importance of discussion.	Seek information. Give information. Review and summarize information.	Ask for suggestions. Listen. Build on suggestions. Decide on plan of action. Determine and assign responsibilities.	Summarize plan of action. Set follow-up date.

VALUES AND ONE TO ONE INTERACTIONS

As mentioned above, leaders in values-driven organizations regularly conduct two types of discussions:

Reinforcing Behavior Consistent with Values

Redirecting Behavior Inconsistent with Values

The four step model . . .

- ◆ Opening
- ◆ Information Sharing
- ◆ Decision
- ◆ Closing

. . . works for both of these types of discussions.

Discussion Guides for Reinforcing Behavior Consistent with Values and Redirecting Behavior Inconsistent with Values follow.

DISCUSSION GUIDE

Reinforcing Behavior
Consistent with Values

BEFORE THE DISCUSSION...

- ♦ Determine exactly why you want to compliment this person.

  - Which value or values are involved?

  - What specifically did he or she do?

AT THE DISCUSSION...

OPENING

- Tell the person you want to offer compliments for acting in a manner which reinforces the organization's values. Be specific. Describe the value and what was done to reinforce it.

- Explain that behaving in a manner consistent with the values results not only in departmental success but it sets a positive example for the entire work team.

INFORMATION SHARING

- Listen to the person's comments. Don't let the person minimize the importance of actions taken. Make sure he or she knows you think it's important.

DECISION

- Ask for suggestions for improving departmental effectiveness. Don't push. Make it clear you are asking because you think he or she is a good performer.

- Explain why you will or won't act on suggestions given.

CLOSING

- Thank the person for the example set by acting in a manner consistent with the values.

- Indicate your intention to act on those suggestions that you think are good ideas.

AFTER THE DISCUSSION...

- ♦ Take whatever steps are necessary to implement the suggestions with which you agree.

DISCUSSION GUIDE

Redirecting Behavior
Inconsistent with Values

BEFORE THE DISCUSSION...

♦ Determine exactly why you want to speak with this person.

• Which value or values are involved?

• What specifically did he or she do or fail to do?

AT THE DISCUSSION...

OPENING

• Tell the person you want to discuss an action which you consider to be in violation of the values.

• Specify the value in question, what the person did, and why you consider this behavior to be in conflict with it.

• Explain that values are guides for everyone's behavior. The result of violating of values is lower productivity and poor morale.

INFORMATION SHARING

• Ask the person for reasons why he or she acted in a manner inconsistent with the values.

• Listen. Summarize the reasons. Show you understand the reasons.

• Emphasize that you expect everyone in the department to act in a manner consistent with the values.

DECISION

• Ask for and obtain the person's commitment to acting in accordance with the values. Explain that you are available to consult on any questions he or she may have regarding the values.

CLOSING

• Thank the person for time given.

• Declare that you are confident future actions will be in a manner consistent with the values.

AFTER THE DISCUSSION...

♦ Make a note to observe this person's behavior.

♦ Actively look for opportunities to compliment this person for acting in a manner consistent with the values.

A Final Word About One to One Discussions

Effective leaders are coaches . . .

. . . not umpires!!!!

One Last Thought . . .

If Our Values are Important Enough to Publish, They are Important Enough to Live By.

Eric Harvey and Al Lucia

CHAPTER 9

In Summary

SUMMARY

The preface of this book promises helpful hints for leaders on how to transform their organizations by using organizational Values to turn their Vision into Reality. When all is said and done, it's quite simple, actually.

SUMMARY

First, leaders must create five conditions within their organizations:

1. Everyone in the organization must understand and accept the values.

2. Everyone in the organization must know how to act in a manner consistent with the values.

3. Everyone in the organization should be recognized and rewarded for acting in a manner consistent with the values.

4. Everyone in the organization must experience negative consequences for acting in a manner inconsistent with the values.

5. There must be no obstacles to acting in a manner consistent with the values.

SUMMARY

Second, to create the conditions necessary for using organizational Values as tools to achieve Vision, leaders must possess and use three skills:

1. Modeling Appropriate Behavior

2. Conducting of Work Group Meetings

3. Interacting One to One

SUMMARY

The majority of this book is devoted to providing
the reader with the knowledge necessary
to put these skills to work. However,
knowledge without action is useless.
The challenge to you, reader, is
to put the knowledge of this
book to work in creating
the kind of organization
you have visualized.

Good Luck

ABOUT THE AUTHOR
BUD BILANICH, EdD

Dr. Bilanich is President of The Organization Effectiveness Group, a consulting firm specializing in improving leadership effectiveness, productivity, quality and service delivery. His unique ability to combine a thorough conceptual understanding of organization theory with a results-oriented, pragmatic approach to problem solving pays big dividends for his clients.

He has 25 years experience in leadership and management training and organizational development. Bud has trained thousands of salespeople, managers and executives. Recently, he developed and implemented a Corporate University, including basic and advanced leadership development programs for a Fortune 500 company. In addition to his training work, he consults with senior executives on leadership effectiveness issues, and the design and implementation of major strategic change initiatives.

He is an internationally known speaker who brings an abundance of energy, wit and insight to his programs. Dr. Bilanich designed the highly acclaimed training programs *Leadership in a Values Driven Organization* and *Superior Sales Management* which are in use in over 40 countries world wide.

Bud has a Doctorate in Adult Education and Organizational Behavior from Harvard University, and an MA in Organization Communication from the University of Colorado. He is listed in *Who's Who in Global Business Leaders* and *Who's Who on CD-ROM*. He is active in the National Speakers Association, American Society for Training and Development, International Association of Business Communicators, and the Association for Quality and Participation. He is the author of *Supervisory Leadership and the New Factory* and *Using Values to turn Vision into Reality*.

You can reach Bud Bilanich at:

The Organization Effectiveness Group
875 South Colorado Boulevard, Suite 773
Denver, CO 80222

Phone   (303) 393-0446
Fax   (303) 393-0081
Email   BUDOEG@aol.com